African-American Heroes

Savion Glover

Stephen Feinstein

Enslow Elementary
an imprint of

Enslow Publishers, Inc.
40 Industrial Road
Box 398
Berkeley Heights, NJ 07922
USA

http://www.enslow.com

Words to Know

choreography (core-ee-OG-ra-fee)—The arrangement of steps in a dance.

classical music—A type of music invented in Europe hundreds of years ago by famous composers.

rhythms (RIH-thums)—Patterns of beats in music.

sole—The bottom of a shoe.

tap dancing—A type of dance using shoes with metal taps on the heels and toes.

Enslow Elementary, an imprint of Enslow Publishers, Inc.

Enslow Elementary® is a registered trademark of Enslow Publishers, Inc.

Copyright © 2009 by Enslow Publishers, Inc.

Library of Congress Cataloging-in-Publication Data

Feinstein, Stephen.
    Savion Glover / Stephen Feinstein.
        p. cm. — (African-American heroes)
    Includes index.
    ISBN-13: 978-0-7660-2897-5
    ISBN-10: 0-7660-2897-6
    1. Glover, Savion—Juvenile literature. 2. Dancers—United States—Biography—Juvenile literature. 3. Choreographers—United States—Biography—Juvenile literature. 4. Tap dancing—United States—History—Juvenile literature. I. Title.
    GV1785.G56F45 2009
    792.802'8092—dc22
    [B]   2007037262

Printed in the United States of America

10 9 8 7 6 5 4 3 2 1

To Our Readers: We have done our best to make sure all Internet Addresses in this book were active and appropriate when we went to press. However, the author and the publisher have no control over and assume no liability for the material available on those Internet sites or on links to other Web sites. Any comments or suggestions can be sent by e-mail to comments@enslow.com or to the address on the back cover.

♻ Enslow Publishers, Inc., is committed to printing our books on recycled paper. The paper in every book contains 10% to 30% post-consumer waste (PCW). The cover board on the outside of each book contains 100% PCW. Our goal is to do our part to help young people and the environment too!

Illustration Credits: AP/Wide World, p. 17; Everett Collection, pp. 3, 9 (upper and lower left), 11, 14, 15, 16 (top), 20; Nic Oatridge/Flickr, pp. 6–7; Getty Images: pp. 1, 2, 3, 5, 9 (upper and lower right), 16 (bottom), 18–19, 21, back cover; Shutterstock, pp. 10, 12.

Cover Illustration: Everett Collection.

Contents

Chapter 1

Born to Dance

Savion Glover was born on November 19, 1973, in Newark, New Jersey. He had two brothers, Carlton and Abron. His mother, Yvette, raised her sons all by herself. Yvette's mother, Anna, lived with them for a while.

One day when Savion was a baby, Grandma Anna was holding him to her shoulder. Savion was crying, and Anna began to hum a song to him. The baby hummed the tune back to her. Anna was so surprised she almost dropped him.

Savion Glover grew up to become a famous tap dancer.

When Savion learned to crawl, he would grab pots and pans from under the kitchen sink. He would bang on them, making up his own **rhythms**.

When Savion began to walk, he went around the house on his tiptoes, like a ballet dancer. He loved to make sounds and was always beating on something.

Savion was born in Newark, New Jersey.

When Savion was four years old, he began to study music at the Newark School of Performing Arts. There he learned how to really play the drums.

When he was six, Savion began playing drums with a band called Three Plus. Two years later, the band was playing at the Broadway Dance Center in Manhattan. There Savion saw the famous tap dancers Lon Chaney and Chuck Green. They were tapping out rhythms as they danced. Savion had never seen such dancing before. And he had never heard such rhythms. Suddenly, he knew that he wanted to be a tap dancer more than anything else.

Sandman
Sims

Honi Coles

Bill
"Bojangles"
Robinson

The Nicholas
Brothers

Savion was inspired by the great
tap dancers of the past.

Chapter 2

The Tap Dance Kid

In 1982, Savion began studying **tap dancing** at the Broadway Dance Center. At first, he wore cowboy boots because they were the only shoes he had with hard **soles**.

Tap dancing became the most important thing in Savion's life. Even when he was not at the Dance Center, he had to dance. Savion danced while he was walking on the street. He danced while he was waiting for the bus. He danced on his bed. He even danced in the shower.

Savion danced everywhere he went.

Savion's tap dancing was all about rhythm and sounds. He used different parts of his feet to make the sounds of different kinds of drums. He used his left heel as a bass drum. He used his right heel as a tom-tom. He made a whip sound like a snare drum with his right toe. He made the crash of the cymbals by stamping both feet flat on the floor. Once Savion got his first real tap shoes, he could dance faster than ever.

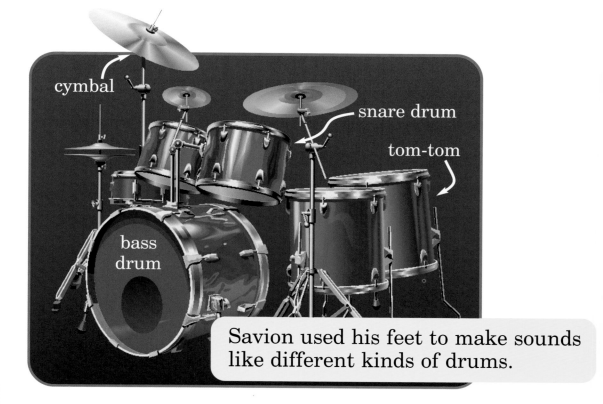

cymbal

snare drum

tom-tom

bass drum

Savion used his feet to make sounds like different kinds of drums.

In 1984, Savion tried out for *The Tap Dance Kid*, a show that was playing on Broadway. It was about a young boy who dreamed of becoming a tap dancer. Savion got the title role. Everyone who saw the show was amazed at his dancing.

One day the great tap dancer Gregory Hines came to watch Savion dance. Hines could hardly believe his eyes. He had never seen a dancer who could tap so fast and so hard. Hines asked Savion to dance in a movie he was making called *Tap*. The next year, Savion began dancing in the children's TV show *Sesame Street*.

Savion dances in his first movie, *Tap*.

Savion with Muppets and kids on *Sesame Street*.

In 1992, Savion and Hines danced together in *Jelly's Last Jam*. The show was about the musician Jelly Roll Morton. Savion learned a lot about tap dancing from Hines. He also learned a lot about life. The two dancers became close friends. Savion saw Hines as the father he never had.

Savion with Gregory Hines in the movie *Tap*.

Savion and Gregory Hines stayed good friends. In this picture, they are dancing together after Savion grew up.

Chapter 4

Savion Keeps Tap Dancing Alive

In 1995 and 1996, Savion danced in a show called *Bring in 'Da Noise, Bring in 'Da Funk*. Savion also did the **choreography** for the show. This means he made up the steps and movements for himself and the other dancers.

Savion made up dances and taught them to other tappers.

Savion and members of his dance group perform in 2003.

In 1997, Savion formed his own dance company called Not Your Ordinary Tappers. Savion began tap dancing to the sounds and rhythms of rap and hip-hop, the music he had grown up with. Savion came up with new steps each time he danced.

After that, Savion danced in many more shows and movies. In 2005, he tap danced to **classical music** in the show *Classical Savion*. The next year, he worked on the movie *Happy Feet*. The people making the movie copied Savion's dancing for Mumble, the tap-dancing penguin.

Savion and the other dancers had their pictures taken with special cameras. Then the pictures were used to make the penguins dance in *Happy Feet*.

Savion's dream was to keep tap alive. When Savion started dancing, tap was not as popular as it used to be. But Savion brought millions of new fans to tap dancing. By always coming up with new and exciting ideas, Savion made his dream come true.

Savion's Own Words

"If I have anything to do with it, tap is going to keep growing. It's going to have its proper place at last."

Timeline

1973—Savion is born in Newark, New Jersey, on November 19.

1980—Savion begins playing drums with the band Three Plus.

1982—Savion begins studying dance at the Broadway Dance Center in Manhattan.

1984—Savion gets the title role in *The Tap Dance Kid*.

1989—Savion appears in the film *Tap*.

1992—Savion dances with Gregory Hines in *Jelly's Last Jam*.

1995–1996—Savion dances in *Bring in 'Da Noise, Bring in 'Da Funk*. He also does the choreography for the show.

1997—Savion forms his own dance company called Not Your Ordinary Tappers.

2005—Savion tap dances to classical music in *Classical Savion*.

2006—Savion dances for the movie *Happy Feet*.

Learn More

Books

Barnes, Lilly. *Toe Tapper*. New York: Somerville House, 1999.

Dillon, Leo and Diane. *Rap a Tap Tap: Think of That!* New York: Blue Sky Press, 2002.

Hasday, Judy L. *Savion Glover: Entertainer*. New York: Chelsea House Publishers, 2006.

Thomas, Mark. *Tap Dancing*. New York: Children's Press, 2001.

Web Sites

Happy Feet

<http://kids.yahoo.com/movies>

Click on "Movies A–Z," then on "H," then on "Happy Feet."

Savion Glover's Official Web Site

<http://www.js-interactive.com/savion>

*I*ndex